Ripley's Believe It or Not!®

Wild & Wacky Edition 2017

SCHOLASTIC

ISBN 978-1-338-11324-2

10 9 8 7 6 5 4 3 2 1   16 17 18 19 20

Printed in the U.S.A.   58
First printing 2016

PUBLISHING

Developed and produced by Ripley Publishing Ltd.

Director, Publishing Operations: Amanda Joiner
Editor: Jessica Firpi
Researcher: Sabrina Sieck
Designers: Shawn Biner, Penny Stamp
Contributors: Jessica Firpi, Margaret Mincks, Jim Steck
Factchecker: Alex Bazlinton
Proofreader: Danny Constantino
Indexer: Johnna VanHoose Dinse
Reprographics: *POST LLC

Pages 26–27

Pages 14–15

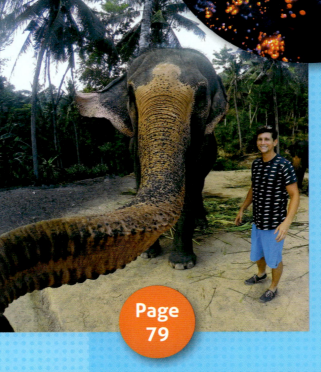

Page 79

Contents

Pages 60–61

Page 23

Page 21

Extra-ODD-inary Legacy

The world of Ripley's Believe It or Not! started with just one iconic man: Robert Ripley. Once the first *Believe It or Not* cartoon was published in the *New York Globe* in 1919, Ripley soon began traveling the world in search of the most unbelievable people and places, visiting more than 200 countries in his lifetime.

He opened his first museum, or Odditorium, in 1933 to showcase all the curious things he had collected on his travels. Ripley also threw himself into radio and television, broadcasting his weird findings from wild locations—even from the bottom of a shark tank!

Today the Ripley's team carries on his legacy, hunting for the best "believe it or nots!" from around the world.

At his peak, Ripley received more than a million letters a year!

Robert Ripley was the first to broadcast from underwater—at the bottom of the shark tank at Marineland in St. Augustine, Florida.

The Ripley cartoons are still drawn every day, making *Ripley's Believe It or Not!* the longest running syndicated cartoon in the world! This cartoon was drawn by Ripley's current cartoonist, John Graziano.

4

To date, there are 32 Ripley's Believe It or Not! Odditoriums around the world, three aquariums, a warehouse packed with incredible artifacts, and an archive of thousands of photos and cartoons.

At Ripley's Aquarium of the Smokies in Gatlinburg, Tennessee, you can meet the Aquarium's playful penguins at the Penguin Encounter or even interact with the stingrays at the Splash with the Stingrays tour!

Searching for the Strange...

Ripley's archivist Edward Meyer, based in our head office in Orlando, Florida, is always on the lookout for the most unique exhibits for all our Ripley's Believe It or Not! Odditoriums. This year he bought some amazing pieces, and these are just some of our favorites straight from the Ripley warehouse.

This figure of Angelina Jolie by Victor Roberto Ramos Licona is made entirely from crayons!

Built by a Thai company, this 22-foot-tall Optimus Prime is made from recycled auto parts.

Created by Gabriel Dishaw, this Dagobah AT-AT sculpture (from the original *Star Wars*® trilogy) is made from recycled computer pieces.

6

Check out these unbelievable stories inside your book...

NO WAY! Keep on an eye out for more Ripley stories and fascinating facts!

Q+A Watch out for interviews inside!

Page 35

Pages 84-85

Page 40

If you have a story you think Ripley's would like, get in touch!

Write to us at: **BION research, Ripley Entertainment Inc., 7576 Kingspointe Parkway, Suite 188, Orlando, Florida, 32819, USA**

Chapter 1

ENTERTAINING ENTERPRISES

State of the Art

Dear Diary

Latvian artist Aniko Kolesnikova makes elaborate journal covers inspired by nature, fantasy, dragons, animals, and birds. Aniko uses polymer clay, a material used in crafts and modeling, to sculpt her fairytale-like creations. Aniko even offers YouTube tutorials to help aspiring artists work their own molding magic.

Tooth-Friendly Treat

Healthy lollipops may sound like a fantasy, but nine-year-old Alina Morse from Michigan made this candy dream a reality. Alina invented ZolliPops®: sugar-free suckers made with Xylitol, Erythritol, Stevia, and other smile-friendly natural ingredients that are actually good for your mouth.

Leaning Tower of LEGO®

In 2013, students from 32 schools across Wilmington, Delaware, spent part of their summer creating an incredible LEGO® tower. At more than 112 feet high and made with over 420,000 LEGO® bricks, the tower held the world record for the tallest structure built with interlocking plastic bricks for a time.

NO WAY!

In November 2014, a road in Shandong, China, was covered in thousands of quilts to prevent it from cracking in cold weather.

ZolliPops®

THE CLEAN TEETH POPS™

Q How did you come up with the idea for ZolliPops?

A I went to the bank with my dad one day and the teller offered me a sucker. My dad always told me that sugar was terrible for my teeth, so I asked, "Why can't we make a sucker that's good for your teeth?" And ZolliPops were born.

Q What is your favorite ZolliPops flavor?

A They all taste great, but I think pineapple is special because most companies don't have a great pineapple-tasting candy. Cherry is new and yummy, too!

Q What has been the hardest part of starting your own business?

A You have to believe and never give up. I asked my dad over a hundred times, "When are we going to make the suckers that are good for you?" Every day has new challenges and opportunities, and you just have to find a way.

Body Canvas

Brazilian photographer Hid Saib creates portraits that really glow. For a recent series titled *Neon*, Hid set up his shoot in a blacked-out studio. Models' faces and shoulders were carefully painted with neon makeup and illuminated by a single ultraviolet light.

Crazy Cups

Coffee Cup Canvas

Carrah Aldridge from Ohio transforms Starbucks coffee cups into amazing works of art! The 20-year-old artist draws on the cups using Sharpies, a white gel pen, and Copic markers to fill in solid areas or to add a gradient.

Five Silly Facts about COFFEE AND TEA

1 Coffee-Powered Car

Martin Bacon converted a Ford pickup truck into the world's fastest coffee-powered vehicle, breaking the land speed record by going 65.5 mph.

2 Tetanus Treatment

Tea made from cockroaches was a traditional remedy for tetanus in 19th-century Louisiana.

3 Caffeine Tech

The first webcam was invented at Cambridge University to check the coffee level of a coffeepot.

4 Fish in My Teacup!

Taiwanese company Charm Villa has created tea bags that look like goldfish when submerged in hot water. The color of the tea inside the bags gives the "fish" their realistic gold tones.

5 Imperial Tea

The most expensive tea in the world, a pot of Da Hong Pao (Imperial Red Robe) is served at the prestigious Royal China Club in London for $250 (£180) — after it has aged for 80 years!

The Art of Cardboard

Boxwars

Established in Melbourne, Australia, in 2003, the annual Boxwars battle sees contenders pit their cardboard creations against each other. Created by Hoss Siegel and Ross Koger, the monumental battle combines art and destruction, with competitors creating battle gear out of recycled cardboard.

In 2004, Australian architect Peter Ryan designed and built a livable house made mostly from cardboard.

Need proof that cardboard is cool? A simple cardboard box is on display in the National Toy Hall of Fame in Rochester, New York.

If the Shoe Fits

Seattle-based artist Michael Leavitt creates original recycled-cardboard shoes. With hand-painted acrylic or enamel, he painstakingly crafts each life-size shoe to look exactly like the original. His "Corrugated Kix" can be worn just like a real shoe—but don't get them wet!

Irrational Rations

Itty-Bitty Brew

Created by Italian goldsmith Pietro Marmo, this tiny coffee maker is just 2 cm (0.8 in) tall—barely bigger than a coffee bean! Composed of five miniature parts, the handcrafted pot takes only 25 seconds to produce a few drops of coffee.

Watermelon Bagels

Bread and butter, cheese and crackers—watermelon and bagels? Japan's Bagel & Bagel restaurant tempts hungry diners with their Suika Bagel ("suika" is Japanese for "watermelon"). The bagels are colored and flavored with watermelon juice and topped with chocolate chip "seeds."

NO WAY! The fizzy sensation and sourness in carbonated beverages come from the carbon dioxide in the drink—not tiny bubbles popping!

Samurai Burgers

In July 2015, Burger King Japan debuted a new menu item called the "AKA Burger" ("aka" meaning "red" in Japanese). Served on red buns and topped with red cheese and red tomatoes, the Samurai Beef and Samurai Chicken burgers are slathered in a spicy sauce made from chili peppers and chili paste called Angry Sauce.

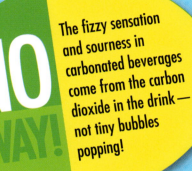

Back to Basics

Moss-Caped Crusader

Send out the Bat-Signal! French artist Christophe Guinet built a funky Batsuit out of foam and pine bark. The suit and its moss cape took about a month to create. Christophe chose pine bark because it was sturdy and easy to find in his area.

Art on Track

In 2011, one Chicago subway car got a mobile makeover courtesy of Mother Nature. Artist Joseph Baldwin and his team of volunteers decorated an El train with lush plants and more than 400 pieces of sod. Baldwin's project, called Art on Track, aimed to raise awareness about environmental responsibility in urban areas.

NO WAY! Artist Jessie Maxwell Bearden makes tasty portraits of celebrities—including the Beatles and Elvis Presley—out of nothing but food!

Ready for Takeoff

MotoArt, a company based in Southern California, is famous for designing furniture out of recycled airplane parts. In 2013, the creative whizzes crafted a conference table from a Boeing 747 Jumbo Jet engine. The 12-foot-wide table features multicolored LED lights, a polished aluminum dome, and a round glass top.

Bake Break

WONKA WEDDING

Ben and Donna Low had a traditional wedding ceremony in South Yorkshire, England, but chose to have a wacky Willy Wonka—themed reception! Bride Donna loves sweets, while groom Ben loves the classic 1971 *Willy Wonka & the Chocolate Factory* film.

SWEET SEND-OFF

Newscast director Mark Herman decided to sweeten his resignation letter—literally. He brought in his sugary letter printed on a white cake with strawberry filling and whipped cream frosting. Knowing his colleagues would be disappointed in his departure, he wanted to find a delicious and hilarious way to break the news.

May 1st, 2015

Dear Michelle,

Please accept this cake as formal (and delicious) notice of my resignation from the position of Newscast Director at KOLD News 13. My last day of employment will be Friday, May 22nd.

I will miss KOLD and all the incredible people I've been fortunate enough to work with over the last 4 years. I cannot thank you enough for all the opportunities and experiences you have given me during my time here.

I appreciate your understanding, and I wish you all the very best. If there's anything I can do to help with the transition during my last few weeks here, please don't hesitate to ask.

Sincerely,

Herman

NO WAY!

A Belgium-based creative agency put a miniature three-bedroom, two-bathroom gingerbread apartment up for sale to raise money for the homeless.

Talent on Toast

Texas-based artist Alfonso Osoria created a sculpture of pop artists Kanye West and Nicki Minaj entirely out of toast. Osoria individually scraped the images into burnt slices of bread and only used bright pink acrylic paint for Nicki's hair.

Fly Hardware

Artist Julie Alice Chappell turns discarded computer circuit boards and electronics into intricate winged insects for her "Computer Component Bugs" collection. Chappell's "bugs" help raise awareness of waste in the environment as well as represent the wonders of modern technology. Based in the United Kingdom, Chappell sells her creations on her popular Etsy shop.

QUIZ

What gift should you get for your birthday?

You're going on vacation! Where would you like to go?

Paris, France

Grand Canyon National Park, Arizona

While at the Grand Canyon, which would you probably be caught doing?

Satisfying my sweet tooth!

I am the real Cookie Monster.

Writing in my journal

Don't want to forget anything!

While in Paris, how do you prefer to get around?

Take public transportation

So much to see, so little time!

Walk

It's the best way to experience the city.

Chapter 2

Bend over

BACKWARD

Get a Leg Up!

Off and Running!

Patrick Sweeney ran 3,355 miles across the United States, crossing 14 states over a period of 114 days—nearly four months! Wearing sandals or, at times, no shoes at all, he made the trip to raise money for charity.

Indiana Jane

Meet Alison Teal, the adventurer who travels the world with her camera, camel, and pink eco surfboard to share the secrets of survival and sustainability. "Indiana Jane," as she is known, has traveled to more than 40 different countries, exploring ancient myths and culture, and has even kissed a cobra!

Leg Rowers of Myanmar

The Intha people of Myanmar have lived on the waters of Inle Lake for generations and have a unique way of fishing: they balance gracefully on one leg and wrap the other leg around the oar to row their boats. With incredible precision, the Intha maneuver their small wooden boats along the channels and floating gardens, using cone-shaped nets to catch fish.

Ski Samurai

Freestyle skier Shogo Kawano knows how to threaten the competition. In 2015, Kawano shunned his ski jacket and wore full samurai armor for a mountain ski race in Japan. His gear weighed a hefty 55 pounds. Kawano also traded his ski poles for a katana—a long, single-edged sword. Now that's slashing the slopes!

Puzzling Pursuits

Ostrich Racing

The Chandler Ostrich Festival in Arizona, celebrating its 28th year, features an unusual pastime: ostrich racing. While the sport may seem a little birdbrained, ostrich racing is nothing new. Historians believe that the Ancient Egyptians were serious ostrich racers, and the practice is still fairly common in parts of Africa.

Your Move

A hybrid fighting sport that combines brains and brawn, chessboxing matches pack more punch! Fighters spar in alternating rounds of chess and boxing, and contestants defeat their opponents with either a checkmate or a knockout.

Bend over Backward

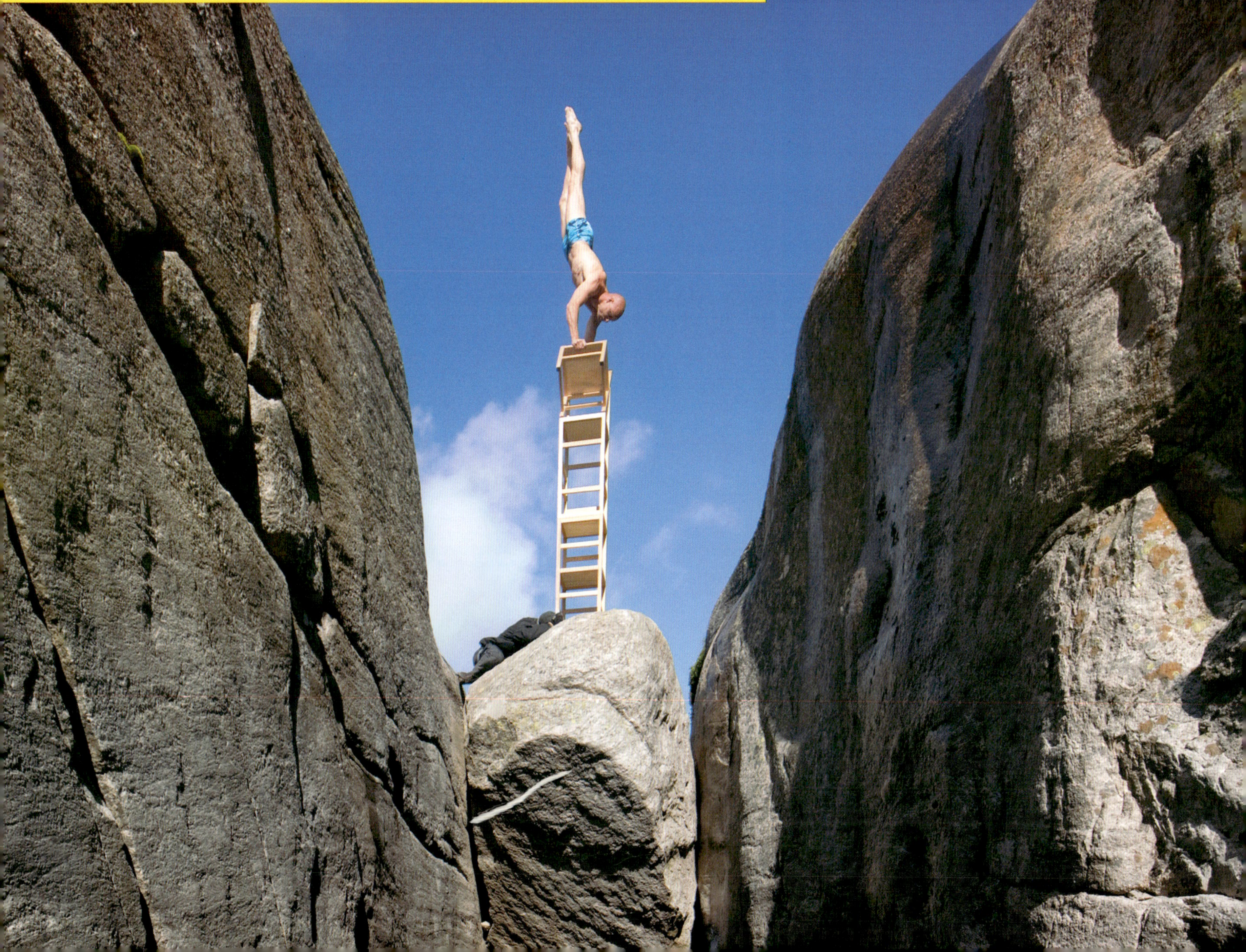

Chairman of the Boulder

Eskil Rønningsbakken, 36, is an extreme artist who travels the world performing potentially lethal balancing acts. In 2009, he performed a handstand on chairs stacked on a rock that bridged a 3,280-foot gap between two Norwegian cliffs.

Way to Be

FRUITY 'DO

A student at the University of Calgary in Canada lost a bet but gained a sweet haircut. Hansel Qiu, 20, and his cousin came up with a bet based on their school and fitness goals. When Hansel's cousin won, she got to shave Hansel's hair however she wanted—which meant a new pineapple look!

Five Wacky Facts about HAIR

1 Hair Sponge

Hair soaks up oil from water, working as a natural sponge, so human hair is used by groups of eco-friendly volunteers to clean up oil spills.

2 Mourning Jewelry

During the Victorian era, jewelry and lockets were made from the hair of deceased loved ones.

3 Growth Speed

The only part of your body that grows faster than hair is bone marrow.

4 Red Nation

The highest concentration of redheads in the world is in Scotland.

5 Common Color

Black hair is the most common hair color.

Take Note

Ben Brucker, a designer for a San Francisco creative agency, felt uninspired by his office's boring décor, so he decided to redecorate, plastering the walls with a series of pixelated superhero portraits made from more than 8,000 Post-it® notes!

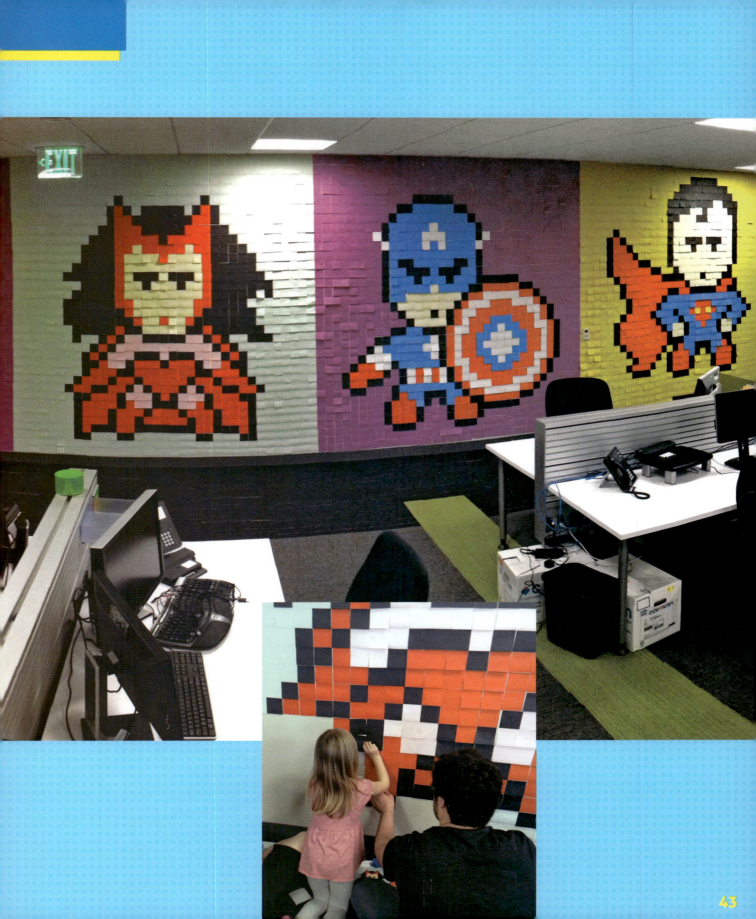

Ashima was listed as one of the 30 Most Influential Teens of 2015 by *TIME*®!

Colossal Climber

Thirteen-year-old Ashima Shiraishi shattered two world records in 10 minutes. In 2015, Ashima completed the highest difficulty rock climb ever performed by a woman, a route dubbed the "Open Your Mind Direct" in Santa Linya, Spain. At one point during the climb, Ashima even hung upside down! At the 2015 World Youth Championships in Arco, Italy, Ashima became the world champion in two disciplines. Now 14, Ashima is one of the top female rock climbers in the world!

Q+A

Q What has been your favorite climb so far, and why?

A My favorite climb so far is "Open Your Mind Direct 9a+" in Spain because it is the climb that made me push my limits to the fullest and reminded me of why I climb!

Q Is there a climb you look forward to completing (or sending)?

A There are many climbs that I hope to send soon. One of them is Terre de Sienne in Hueco Tanks, Texas.

Q How long does it typically take to finish a climb?

A Usually a project takes me 4 to 7 days to finish — which is very fast, but there are some climbs that I still haven't accomplished after years.

Q Is there any special victory food you like to eat after sending?

A My celebratory treat usually depends on where I am. For example, when I recently won the World Youth Championships in Italy, I got four scoops of amazing gelato! But it's usually cookies, cakes, or gelato!

Q Besides climbing, what do you like to do for fun?

A Since I'm also a teenager, I like to watch movies and YouTube videos, and I'm a huge foodie!

When climbers "send," it means they've cleanly and successfully completed a route.

Sporting Youth

GUTSY GOLFER

Four-year-old Tommy Morrissey of Palm Beach, Florida, was born without a fully developed right arm. Tommy nicknamed his arm "Nemo" after the Disney fish with the famously small fin—but there's nothing tiny about Tommy's impressive golf swing. Tommy can drive a ball nearly 100 yards with only his left arm!

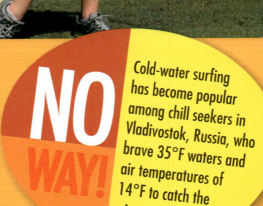

NO WAY! Cold-water surfing has become popular among chill seekers in Vladivostok, Russia, who brave 35°F waters and air temperatures of 14°F to catch the wintry waves.

Jenna vs. Tuna

Twelve-year-old Jenna Gavin of Nova Scotia, Canada, pulled off an impressive marine feat. In 2014, the feisty fisherwoman caught a 618-pound bluefin tuna in Canada's Northumberland Strait, setting a new world record for her age group. Jenna battled the bluefin for nearly two hours before reeling it in without any help. Jenna's reward for landing the big fish? A new iPad mini, courtesy of her proud parents.

Tractor Tricks

Ten-year-old Ratanjith Patil from Sangli, Maharashtra, India, has already found his passion—driving and performing jaw-dropping tractor stunts without any safety gear. Ratanjith first learned how to drive when he was just in kindergarten, but now he is a master behind the wheel of the family tractor.

7250 DI MASSEY FERGUSON

POWER PAANCH
TRIMBAXLE

Modern Mayhem

In Southern France, modern knights still practice the medieval sport of jousting, but there's a twist—competitors ride boats instead of horses. This splashy sport, officially called water jousting or marine jousting, can be traced back to ancient Egypt. Water jousting tournaments continue today on rivers and canals across France.

NO WAY!

Even at the age of 71, Ron Long of Wales, who calls himself the "Old Tosser," can skip a stone across water further than 300 feet at almost 90 miles per hour.

Ville de Sète

QUIZ

Who should you be friends with?

It's a Saturday afternoon. What are you most likely doing?

Watching TV or reading a book inside

Playing sports or exercising outdoors

You're doodling in your notebook. What are you most likely drawing?

Something intricately patterned and SUPER colorful!

My favorite superhero (as best I can, anyway)!

Are you afraid of heights?

No, I don't mind heights

Yes, even elevators freak me out

page 46
Jenna Gavin and her giant tuna

page 40
Pineapple head

page 43
Dude that decorated his office with 8,000 Post-its®

page 44
Ashima Shiraishi (best female rock climber in the world)

Chapter 3

Bizarre World

Natural Sights

Hundreds of trees in a forest near Gryfino, Poland, are mysteriously bent at the bottom!

CRYSTAL CHAMBERS

Located in Chihuahua, Mexico, the Cueva de los Cristales, or Cave of Crystals, contains the largest selenite crystals ever found. Thought to be 500,000 years old, the cave sits above a magma chamber and maintains a temperature of nearly 120°F.

Glass Beach

In MacKerricher State Park, near Fort Bragg, California, lies Glass Beach, where decades of dumping garbage into the coastline area has created rare and beautiful sea glass. Sea glass is created when raw glass is broken into smaller pieces, slowly polished by the sand, and rounded by the rolling waves. Thousands of tourists visit Glass Beach every year, but collecting the precious sea glass is discouraged.

The edge of Niagara Falls is constantly moving and will eventually disappear into Lake Erie!

At the bottom of the deepest point on Earth, the Mariana Trench, the water pressure is equivalent to 100 elephants standing on your head!

Frosted Fun!

FIGHTING THE FROST

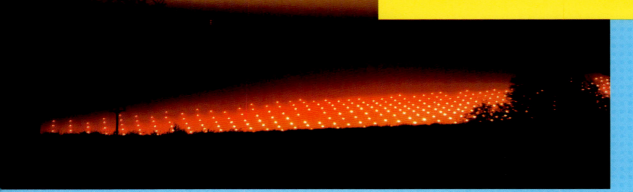

The Waitrose Leckford Estate vineyard in Hampshire, England, has a powerful enemy: frost. To protect vines from this chilly foe, a team of three people work through the night during chilly seasons placing 750 candles on the ground. The candles help raise the surrounding temperature, keeping frost at bay.

SLUSHY SURF

One blustery day in 2015, photographer Jonathan Nimerfroh spotted a strange sight on the Nantucket, Massachusetts, beach: half-frozen waves. Dubbed "Slurpee waves," the slushy, chilly crests rolled ashore in 19°F weather.

WINTER PLAYGROUND

Many playgrounds are abandoned during the winter, but not the winter playground in Kiruna, Sweden. Built in 2015, the playground was made entirely from snow and ice, featuring a giant maze, two slides, a huge snow lantern, four egg-shaped seats, and icy benches.

NO WAY!

Featuring jousting knights, a giant chess set, ice chandeliers, and polar bear bedrooms, the Aurora Ice Museum in Alaska is the largest year-round ice environment in the world.

Hang Tight

Skylodge, a high-hanging hotel overlooking Peru's Sacred Valley, is not your typical overnight stay. Skylodge visitors stay in see-through pods on the side of a cliff. Gutsy guests can hike the cliff, zoom across a zip wire, or climb a 400-foot steel ladder to reach their rooms.

Dirty Thunderstorm

In April 2015, German photographer Adrian Rohnfelder shot this stunning image of a dirty thunderstorm over the southern peak of Sakurajima, known as Minamidake. One of the most consistently active volcanoes in Japan, Sakurajima's dirty thunderstorm (or volcanic lightning) is a rare weather phenomenon created by electrical charges generated when rock fragments, ash, and ice particles in a volcanic plume collide.

Arctic Holidays

In 2012, Daniel Gray spent the holidays with his girlfriend, Kat Starrie, and her family in Edmonton, Canada. Kat's mother, Brigid, challenged them to build an igloo using milk cartons. Over the course of five days and in −13°F weather, Daniel and Kat dyed, froze, and arranged between 500 and 700 ice blocks into a colorful dome.

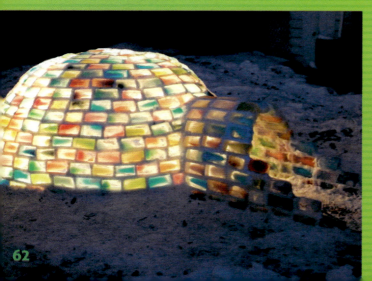

Q+A

Q Did you already have all the milk cartons ready? How long did it take to save the cartons?

A When I arrived in Edmonton early in December, Brigid [my girlfriend's mother] had already done most of the collecting. She had been doing it for around three months and had been getting workmates and local coffee shops to contribute.

Q How much time did you spend designing the igloo?

A We spent around a week just looking at the logistics of building an igloo. There was a great video done by the National Film Board of Canada that gave us some information, including the spiral structure of the igloo. We also had another engineer around for afternoon tea to discuss ideas.

Q What was the hardest part about creating the igloo?

A We didn't really know how to stick the blocks together, and we eventually started using what we called "snowcrete." We got big tubs of snow and then some hot water and mixed it up. This acted as a really good mortar. Another difficulty was trying to get the right tilt on the blocks to get the dome shape.

Q How did you guys celebrate after the igloo was completed?

A We hosted an igloo party where neighbors, family, and friends were invited to come and have a look. There were lots of Arctic-themed nibbles: seal sweets, whale jerky (muktuk), caribou gold, walrus nuggets, polar bear oysters, Arctic hare bites, musk oxen minis, Arctic fox treats, and Arctic shrimp.

More than You Can Chew

So Stuffed!

In July 2015, Yawarakan's Café opened in Tokyo, Japan, catering only to stuffed animals—those with a reservation, that is! The animals are mailed in overnight and treated to a main course of rice omelet—cooked by the restaurant "owner," Karei, a stuffed animal flounder—along with coffee and a delicious stack of 10 pancakes with maple syrup for dessert. After chowing down, the stuffed animals listen to ghost tales and play cards before going to sleep. The nonhumans then get mailed back home, but not without souvenirs and a photo album to commemorate their fun time!

Cutting Ties

For 58 years, Pinnacle Peak Patio Steakhouse in Scottsdale, Arizona, enforced a strict policy: no ties allowed. Their casual dress code meant business. Pinnacle employees snipped off more than 1,000,000 ties from diners who dared to defy them. The cut ties hung as decoration from the steakhouse's ceiling.

Mas Provencal, a restaurant near Nice, France, is a unique eatery where nearly every inch is adorned with fresh flowers and plants. Diners can even nosh on grapes and cherry tomatoes hanging from the ceiling.

At the Disaster Café in Lloret del Mar, Spain, thrill-seeking diners can chow down during a simulated earthquake. Tip: Wear a bib.

BEWARE

WEAR TIES AT YOUR OWN RISK

Out of Place

Hungry Sinkhole

In May 2010, Tropical Storm Agatha pounded Guatemala City, Guatemala, with torrential rain and mudslides, causing the collapse of a massive sinkhole. The hole, which measured about 60 feet wide and swallowed an entire three-story building, may have been months or years in the making.

Five Insane Facts about NATURAL DISASTERS

1 Hurricane Names

Hurricanes were first given names by Australian meteorologist Clement Wragge (1852-1922), who named violent storms after politicians he disliked.

2 Volcanic Eruptions

There are between 10 and 20 active volcanoes erupting right at this very moment.

3 Moonquakes

The moon has regular "moonquakes"—some reading more than 5 on the Richter scale!

4 Sunflower Power

Thousands of sunflowers were planted at the site of the 1986 Chernobyl nuclear disaster in Ukraine because they absorb radioactive material through their roots.

5 Oak Smoke

Oak trees are more likely to be hit by lightning than any other type of tree.

Cave of Wonders

Located in Quang Binh Province, Vietnam, Hang Son Doong is the largest cave in the world. At more than 656 feet high, 492 feet wide, and three miles long, the cave even has its own jungle, river, and climate. It was originally found by a local man in 1991 but was recently rediscovered in 2009. The name "Hang Son Doong" means "mountain river cave."

NO WAY! Stalactites and stalagmites can eventually join from floor to ceiling; however, they grow very slowly—some only about an inch every 100 years!

Timeless Travels

ALIEN ISLAND

Described as "the most alien place on Earth," the remote island of Socotra in the Indian Ocean is home to 800 rare species of flora and fauna, a third of which cannot be seen anywhere else on the planet. The trees and plants—including the dragon blood tree, whose red resin was used in medieval magic—have evolved to adapt to the hot, dry climate.

Who's There?

No need to knock! The Indian village of Shani Shingnapur—including homes, schools, banks, and most public toilets—is almost completely doorless. Local legend has it that the deity Shani protects villagers from danger, making doors unnecessary.

NO WAY!

In 1990 a flight attendant hung on to a pilot who was sucked out of the broken windscreen of a jumbo jet at 17,300 feet until the plane landed!

Trampoline Road

Visitors to the 2012 Archstoyanie Art Festival in Nikola-Lenivets, Russia, were able to bounce along a 170-foot-long trampoline road built through the middle of a forest. Made from reinforced rubber, the road, called Fast Track, was designed by a team of Estonian architects who wanted to explore new and fun ways of getting from one place to another.

QUIZ

Where in the world should you visit?

What activity do you enjoy doing the most?

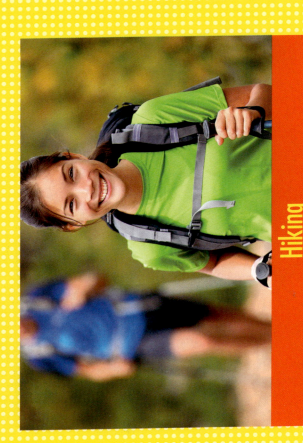

Hiking

Swimming

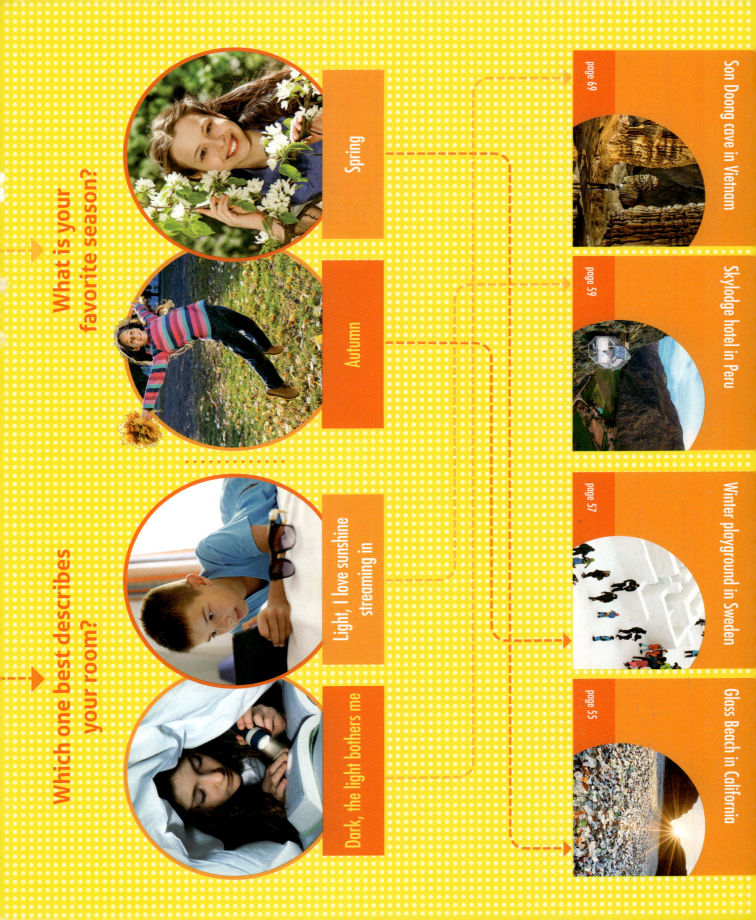

What is your favorite season?

Spring

Autumn

Which one best describes your room?

Light, I love sunshine streaming in

Dark, the light bothers me

Son Doong cave in Vietnam
page 69

Skylodge hotel in Peru
page 59

Winter playground in Sweden
page 57

Glass Beach in California
page 55

Chapter 4

Funky Fauna

Heart and Soul

LOVE BIRD

Photographer Ingrid Bunse was taking pictures of storks performing a mating dance in Kruger National Park, South Africa, when she was stunned to see this bird seemingly bursting with love—with his bright-red heart on his chest.

MOBILE REPTILE

Lots of pets love fresh air, and Bon-chan the giant African tortoise is no exception. Owner Hisao Mitani takes Bon-chan on regular (and very slow) strolls through the streets of Tokyo, Japan. Sometimes the 150-pound pet even sports cool costumes!

Camera Ready

FIERCE PHOTO

Beauty meets beast in an astounding series of underwater images by Australian photographer Jeremy Ferris. The shoot, which took place in oceans all over the world, features models and divers posing with whale sharks, tiger sharks, hammerheads, and more!

NO WAY!

Rambo, an octopus at a New Zealand aquarium, is trained to press a camera's shutter button when visitors stand in front of a backdrop.

Elephant Selfie

Christian LeBlanc of Vancouver, Canada, was feeding a friendly elephant while on vacation in Thailand when suddenly the elephant reached for Christian's camera with his trunk. Since the camera was set to film continuously, the elephant captured the twosome in one amazing selfie — or as Christian called it, an "elphie"!

Pump It Up

You might have heard of gym rats, but what about gym squirrels? In a supremely silly shoot, photographer Max Ellis captured some furry friends pumping iron. Max first hung weights with fishing wire and then gave the squirrels treats to tempt them into workout poses.

What's Bugging You?

Alien Butt Spider

Widespread along Australia's east coast, the *Araneus praesignis* spider has two "eyes" on its back that make it look like the face of an alien! A type of orb weaver, the spider is more commonly known as an alien butt spider. The eyes on its back are used to confuse predators, helping the nocturnal spider escape to safety.

Five Wacky Facts about BUGS

1 Insect-Licious

Since creepy crawlies are an excellent source of protein, minerals, and vitamins, a company named Crowbar Protein worked with a chef to create delicious "insect-powered protein bars" made with cricket flour, nuts, dates, and cinnamon.

2 Dust Eaters

Up to one-third of the weight of a pillow can be made up of dead skin... and tiny arachnids called dust mites, their poop, and the bacteria that feeds on the poop! Dust mites do a great job of eating the dead skin that falls off your body while you sleep.

3 Smelly Disguise

Did you know that bird dung spiders disguise themselves as bird poop?

4 Weta Sight!

Measuring as long as four inches (not including the legs and antennae), the giant weta is one of the heaviest insects, with one captive weta weighing in at 2.5 ounces—heavier than a sparrow!

5 Save the Queen!

If a queen leafcutter ant dies, so do all the other ants in her colony.

Close Encounters

Open Wide

Most people make an appointment with their dentist for healthy teeth — but not Russell Laman! While snorkeling in Bali in 2013, 13-year-old Russell simply imitated the fish around him, convincing a white banded cleaner shrimp to swim into his mouth for a quick polish!

Monster Lobster

Pacific spiny lobsters rarely weigh more than three pounds due to overfishing—but in 2014, a lobster found off the coast of Santa Barbara, California, tipped the scale at a whopping 12 pounds! The lobster, nicknamed "Albert Girther," is thought to be an impressive 70 years old!

Safari Survivor

In 2010, a male Masai giraffe broke his neck in a fight and somehow managed to survive without any medical attention. Years later, the tough giraffe now sports what appears to be a zigzag neck. He has adjusted well to life at Serengeti National Park in Tanzania, taking his food from low-hanging trees where he can reach.

Krupa nicknamed the squirrel supermodel "Sneezy" because she tends to sneeze while sniffing around for nuts.

Squirrel Whisperer

Meet Sneezy, one of Penn State University's many eastern gray squirrels. With the help of some peanuts, Sneezy allows photographer and "squirrel whisperer" Mary Krupa to get close enough to pet her, dress her in costumes, and snap some adorable photos!

We asked Mary how she gets Sneezy ready for her close-ups!

Q When did you first meet Sneezy?

A During my freshman year, I discovered that the campus squirrels, used to being fed by people, were extremely friendly. Some would even allow themselves to be touched — in exchange for food, of course. I thought, "If the squirrel lets me touch her, maybe she will tolerate having a doll's hat put on her head" — and fortunately, I was right!

Q Did you have to tame Sneezy, or was she initially friendly?

A She is a wild animal, but she's the calmest, most trusting squirrel I've ever met. Once she saw that I had food for her, she didn't hesitate to come right up and "ask" for some. Within minutes, she was letting me gently stroke her head. A few weeks later, she would happily eat while perched in the palm of my hand.

Q If you could make ANY costume for Sneezy, no matter how expensive or time-consuming, what would it be?

A I think she'd look dashing in a tiny fedora. Or maybe in a little jeep, going on a safari! Some tiny goggles for scuba diving, perhaps? The possibilities are endless!

Q Do you have any other furry friends, or are you squirrel-exclusive?

A I love all animals, but, along with squirrels, birds are a particular favorite of mine. I share my home with a perky parakeet named Smudge, who loves to perch on my head.

Reindeer Wranglers

The isolated Dukha (or Tsaatan) tribe of northern Mongolia has a strong spiritual connection to reindeer. Photographer Hamid Sardar-Afkhami captured this special bond between man and beast. The tribe breeds and domesticates reindeer, using them for milk, cheese, and fur. The Dukha people also ride the reindeer to hunt wild elk and boar. Sadly, the reindeer population is declining, threatening the Dukha's unique way of life.

Stuck in a Trap

Measuring as much as five feet in diameter and built up to six feet above ground, the conjoined web of female red-legged golden orb spiders is so large and is woven from such strong silk that it can ensnare bats and even birds. This bird—a seafaring lesser noddy—became trapped in a web on Cousine, an island in the Seychelles. Luckily for the bird, it was saved before it was too late.

A woodpecker's tongue can be as long as its body. It even has a barb on the end of it for skewering grubs.

Paw-Stars

In July 2015, the Hallmark Channel aired the first-ever *Paw Star Game*, where tiny kittens played baseball on a tiny baseball diamond. Celebrities like Al Roker and Mario Lopez joined in the event, which helped more than 90 kittens get adopted.

Snap 'Em Up!

On one episode of Price Is Right, an elephant was offered as a "bonus prize." The contestant won and insisted on the prize instead of the $4,000, and a live elephant from Kenya had to be delivered to him.

CRAB DISPENSER

A food vending machine in Nanjing, China, sells live crabs. Designed by Shi Tuanjie, the machine offers live hairy crabs and accompanying bottles of vinegar. The crabs, a tasty delicacy in the region, vary in price according to size and are packed into plastic boxes and chilled to 40°F, leaving them sedated but still alive.

Actual Size
1.5 inches

Blue Dragon

Found throughout the world's oceans in temperate and tropical waters, the *Glaucus atlanticus* is a tiny sea slug commonly known as the blue dragon. Its striped skin serves as camouflage, blending in with the blue of the water as it floats on the ocean's surface belly-up. It can only grow up to 1.5 inches in length, but don't be fooled! This little slug feeds on venomous animals like the much larger Portuguese man-of-war, and it saves venom in its fingerlike appendages.

In the United Kingdom, all horses, ponies, and donkeys must have a horse passport.

QUIZ

What crazy critter are you?

You're in the middle of house hunting. Which house will you get?

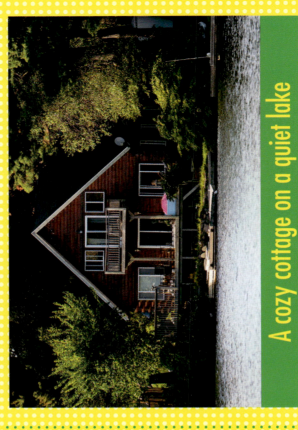

A cozy cottage on a quiet lake

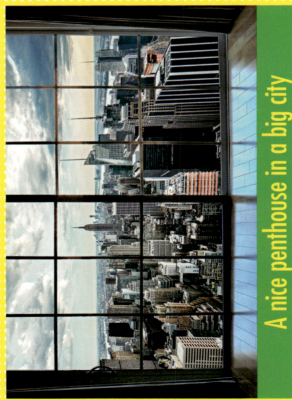

A nice penthouse in a big city

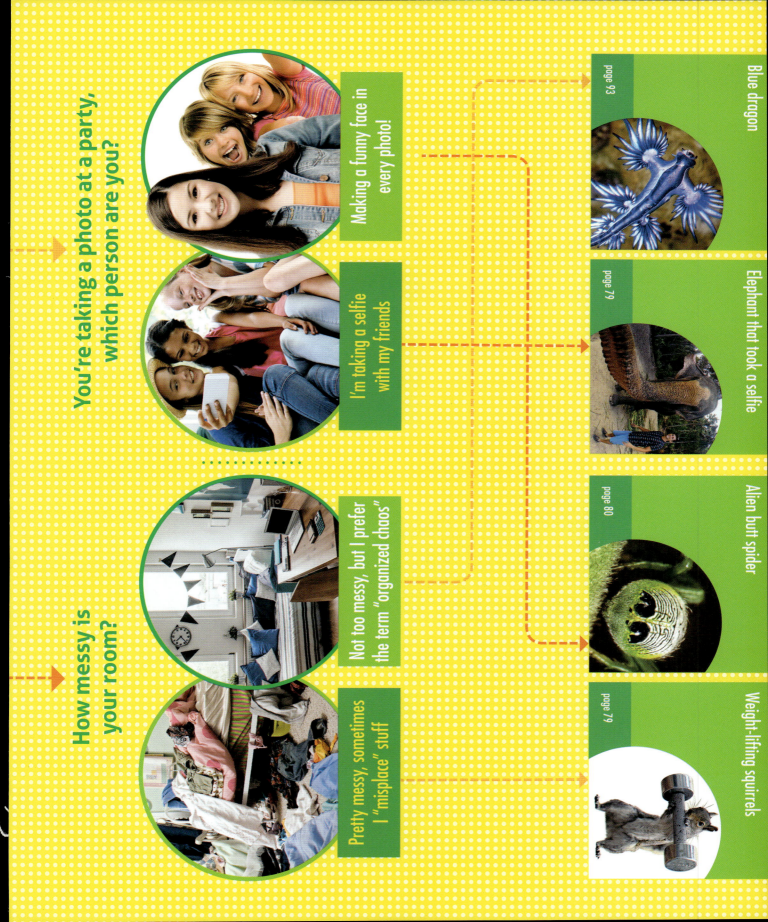

Chapter 5

CROSS YOUR

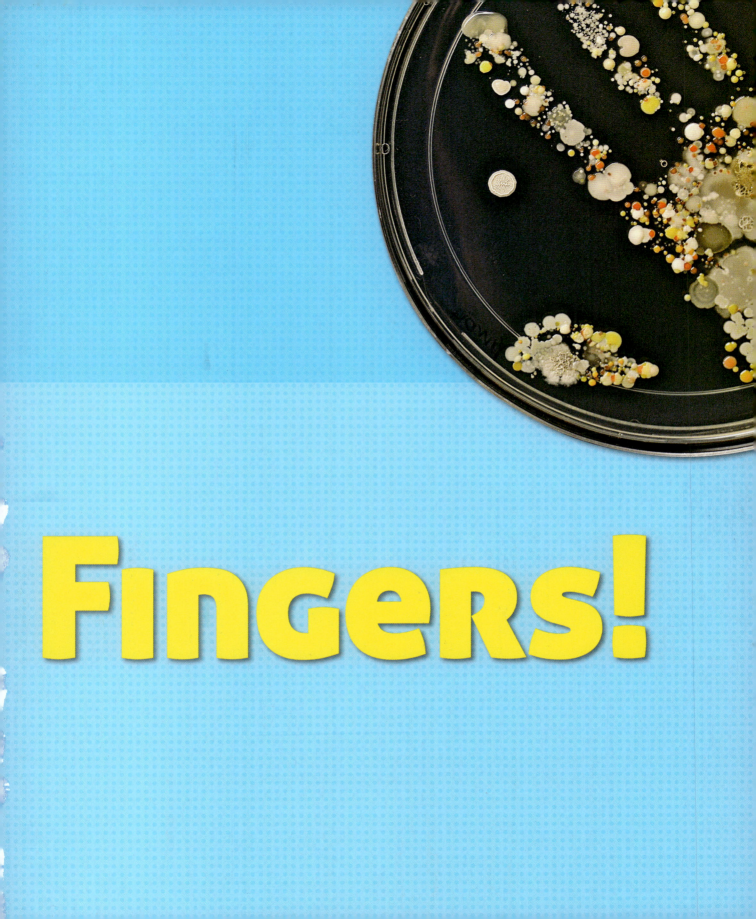

Fingers!

NO WAY!

With the "Skin Book," tattoo artists can now practice designs before working on a real person. The book has synthetic pages that feel like actual human skin!

Rethinking Ink

In Myanmar's Chin State, some older women sport full-face tattoos. According to legend, the practice began to keep foreign princes away from Chin women. Later the tattoos became a symbol of beauty, strength, and cultural pride. To create the elaborate designs, ink is hammered into the skin with a thorn similar to a pine needle. Today, the tattoos are banned by the government.

Water World

The Bajau people of Malaysia spend almost their entire lives at sea. Refugees from the Philippines, the Bajau are forbidden from coming ashore. They live in wooden huts on stilts and survive by catching seafood in their handmade boats. Some Bajau people even experience "ground sickness" when they leave the water, similar to seasickness for those who live on land.

Bold Bodies

Chemical engineer Dave Whitlock has not bathed in 12 years. Instead, he sprays his skin with a mist of live bacteria!

RARE TRIUMPH

Army veteran Kirk Mount enjoys the thrill of extreme sports — despite being confined to a wheelchair. The 28-year-old is paralyzed from the waist down but never lets that stop him from performing outdoor feats like cliff diving and hill climbing.

Jessica Cox from Tucson, Arizona, can fly an airplane, surf, play the piano, and has a black belt in Tae Kwan Do—all without arms! In 2008, Jessica became the world's first licensed armless pilot.

Fearless Fisherman

Clay Dyer, a professional bass fisherman, was born with no legs, no left arm, and only part of a right arm. Still, he uses no special aids in competition. Clay wedges the rod between his neck and shoulder, twists his body to drop the line, and reels in a catch with his partial right arm.

Guilty Pleasures

TOXIC TRICKS

Tian Jiashi from Changchun, China, divides his time between teaching dance and shocking audiences by swallowing venomous animals. Tian has given thousands of performances with his deadly pets, admitting that he's been bitten and stung hundreds of times, sometimes seriously. The 33-year-old—who prefers snakes, scorpions, and centipedes—raises all the animals himself at home, using the money he makes from his shows to look after his toxic friends and add more to his collection.

Two-Face

Michigan artist James Kuhn has completed over 365 days of face painting! Kuhn's imaginative designs are different every day and range from cartoon characters to some of his favorite foods. He says the worst part is painting the insides of his nostrils. Check out these crazy designs!

If the human eye was a digital camera, it would have 576 megapixels.

Yawning doesn't wake us up, but it helps us regulate the temperature of our brains.

105

Inno-Ventions

MUSIC TO MY EARS

In a new wave of technology, swimmers can now listen to music underwater by using Neptune headphones. The waterproof headphones and MP3 player vibrate sound through a swimmer's cheekbones, mimicking the way whales and dolphins communicate underwater. In the end, it makes a swimmer feel like the music is playing inside his or her head!

Five Zany Facts about INVENTIONS

1 Microwave Melt

American engineer Percy Spencer invented the microwave oven after a candy bar melted in his pocket as he stood next to a radar tube.

2 Easy on the Ears

Earmuffs were invented by a 15-year-old American boy in the 19th century!

3 Swim Fins

Benjamin Franklin invented swim fins—for hands!

4 Start Your Engines!

If water were pumped through the Space Shuttle Main Engines (SSMEs) instead of fuel, the three engines could drain an average family-sized swimming pool in 25 seconds.

5 First Vending Machine

Roughly 2,000 years ago, engineer Hero of Alexandria (Heron Alexandrinus) invented the first vending machine. It dispensed holy water!

Hair Violin

London-based artist Tadas Maksimovas had been growing his hair for 10 years before deciding he wanted to do something creative when he cut it off. Enlisting the help of one of Lithuania's most famous violinists, Eimantas Belickas, Tadas decided to twist his 2.6-foot-long hair into violin strings and have Eimantas play the violin—while the hair was still attached to his head.

Q What was the hardest part of the experiment?

A It took me two years to turn the idea into a reality mainly because I couldn't find anyone who would agree to help me in making the violin strings. One day I got frustrated and called one of the best Lithuanian violin players, Eimantas Belickas, and he loved my idea!

Q How long did the entire experiment take?

A We used superglue for the strings/hair to make it harder and into one solid piece rather than many separate threads. It took about half an hour for each string to be made because we had to wait until the glue dried out completely. When that was done, Eimantas strung the strings on the violin. It took about half an hour to get into tune and about an hour to shoot it.

Q Did the process hurt at all?

A My hair roots are really sensitive, and I couldn't even allow anyone to brush my hair. So while Eimantas played, I had to remind him from time to time not to pull the violin too hard. It was a bizarre feeling as well—not because of the sound, but because of the way we looked.

Cross Section Creations

To Lisa Nilsson, the human body is a work of art. Lisa makes amazing anatomical cross sections using rolled paper, a technique called "quilling." She starts with a photograph of an actual cross section of a body part and then begins pinning small rolls of paper.

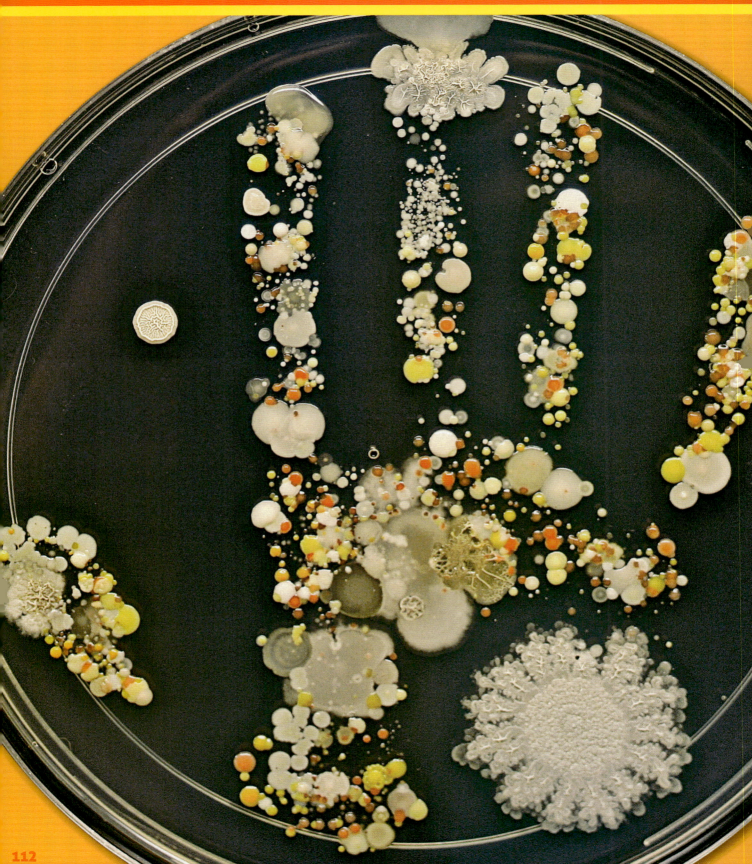

Wash Your Hands

Who says bacteria can't be beautiful? Tasha Sturm, a microbiology lab technician, thought her kids might be interested in seeing the microorganisms on their hands, so she made it a project. First Tasha built a giant Petri dish. After her son pushed his hand into the dish, she covered it and let it sit for four days. The result was a colorful microorganism collage!

© Tasha Sturm

Clever Efforts

In a bid to convince people to stop smoking, a Thai health group made ink from the lungs of longtime smokers.

UV TATTOO

Californian tattoo artist Richie Streate specializes in ultraviolet (UV) tattoos. Once the scarring heals after about a year, the tattoos are completely invisible in regular light—but they come to life under UV light!

HAIR INSECTS

Artist Adrienne Antonson from Asheville, North Carolina, bends and weaves real human hair into remarkably detailed insect artworks, using glue to mold the hair and to hold it in place. Adrienne collects hair from close friends and family. She wants to use her creations for art therapy, working with people who have lost their hair through illness.

Since January 2011, the Belly Button Biodiversity project has been investigating the microbes that inhabit our belly buttons!

QUIZ

What crazy talent would you be best at?

How would your friends describe you?

Quiet and chill

Fearless and sporty

You're late for class!
How do you make it before the bell rings?

I run as fast as I can!

I don't, but I try to make sure the teacher doesn't see me come in late!

It's time to choose an elective class.
Which would you choose?

Art

Music

page 105

Crazy James Kuhn face paint!

page 109

Playing the violin with hair!

page 102

Extreme sports like Kirk Mount!

page 111

Cross section art!

Chapter 6

Culture Collection

Superstars!

SUPER MAKEUP

Clark Kent used a phone booth to turn into Superman. Lianne Moseley has her own secret weapon: Aquacolor makeup. Lianne, a professional makeup artist from Canada, transforms everyday people into comic book superheroes. Her astonishing creations, including Superman, Aquaman, Spock, and Gambit, can take up to seven hours to complete.

Marvel-ous

Xing Yile, a 26-year-old middle school art teacher in Zhengzhou, China, built replicas of the Iron Man suit and Hulkbuster armor to celebrate the release of Disney's *Avengers: Age of Ultron*. A megafan of the Marvel superhero films, Xing spent two months with an assistant making the full-scale models. The 11-foot-tall Hulkbuster armor weighed half a ton and was made up of 100 fiberglass parts.

Noel Cruz repaints celebrity dolls to make them look more like the real thing. He restyles the doll's hair, removes existing paint from the doll's face, and then redraws and repaints facial features, using photographs for reference.

Inventor Patrick Priebe created a fully functional Iron Man glove that can shoot actual lasers.

Crafting Quality

In 2014, Swedish 3-D artist Caroline Eriksson combined a holiday classic with literature and movies. Caroline whipped up a giant gingerbread sculpture of Smaug, the fictional dragon from J. R. R. Tolkien's *The Hobbit*. The towering treat took two weeks to complete, requiring extra syrup and flour to support the dragon's weight. Caroline later created a gingerbread Optimus Prime from the *Transformers* movies.

Hit the Road

NICE RIDE

Young Molly Wickenden travels in style. Her dad drives her to school in an exact replica of the DeLorean from the movie *Back to the Future*. The Wickendens' model, built by Universal Studios, features details from the movie car including a flux capacitor, an energy reactor, and neon lights.

> The Wind Explorer, a kite-powered hybrid-electric car, traveled 3,100 miles across Australia using only $15 worth of electricity!

Charitable Car

Anna and Elsa would surely take a spin in this fantastic *Frozen*-themed car. The icy automobile comes courtesy of Kristian Ek and Niklas Sahlin of Sweden. The duo gave Kristian's BMW E46 a frosty makeover all in the name of charity, donating funds raised to a Swedish cancer foundation.

American commuters will spend more than two months of their lives stuck in traffic!

In August 2013, a woman from New Zealand drove more than 180 miles at night while asleep and had no memory of the trip!

Choosing the Music

Rock On

Part of The National GUITAR Museum and built to demonstrate the principles of acoustics, the mammoth Gibson Flying V is the world's largest playable guitar. At nearly 45 feet long and 16 feet wide, the guitar weighs 2,255 pounds — as much as a compact car!

Five Silly Facts about **MUSIC**

1 Musical Skateboards

Juhana Nyrhinen from Finland makes $500 electric versions of traditional stringed Finnish folk instruments from ordinary skateboards.

2 Feline Refrain

Two psychologists at the University of Wisconsin—Madison and a composer at the University of Maryland teamed up to make songs specifically for cats.

3 iTunes Record

Louie Sulcer, 71, from Woodstock, Georgia, received a personal phone call from Steve Jobs and a $10,000 gift card after buying the 10 billionth track downloaded from iTunes in 2010.

4 Cassette Dress

Texan artist Alyce Santoro makes clothes from stitched cassette tapes, which will still play sounds if you run a cassette player head over the fabric!

5 Melodic Help

A team of Canadian researchers found that playing music to premature babies reduced their pain levels and encouraged better feeding habits, which in turn helped with weight gain.

Bathroom Business

Quacky Collection

Rubber ducks aren't just child's play. Rinat Matityahu, 37, of England has been building her toy flock for nearly a decade. Rinat, who says she's spent thousands on ducks, proudly owns more than 3,000 bathtub buddies. Her favorite duck-hunting spot? German eBay.

NO WAY!

To help keep public spaces clean, Mexican Internet company Terra introduced a machine called Poo Wi-Fi. This smelly innovation offers free Wi-Fi in exchange for dog poop.

Lather Up

Do you eat, sleep, and breathe video games? Why not bathe with them, too? Digital Soaps owner Chrystal Doucette from Bellingham, Washington, shapes soaps in the form of PlayStation controllers, Nintendo cartridges, and *Portal 2*'s Companion Cube. If you're game, Chrystal also sells soap Rubik's Cubes.

Totally Gaudi

San Francisco's Granny's Cottage, also known as Granny's Empire of Art, has ten themed rooms designed by various artists. The bathroom, dubbed Gaudi Submarine, makes a splash with its funky underwater vibe. The wacky water closet pays tribute to the Beatles and Spanish architect Antoni Gaudi, featuring colorful mosaics of sea creatures, porthole windows, a yellow submarine bathtub, and a copper periscope!

X-traordinary

Spike Vain, a veterinary oncology technician in Los Angeles, California, had been collecting her patients' X-rays, CT scans, and MRIs for years before she got a light-bulb idea combining art and science. Now Spike creates incredible lampshades from animal X-rays!

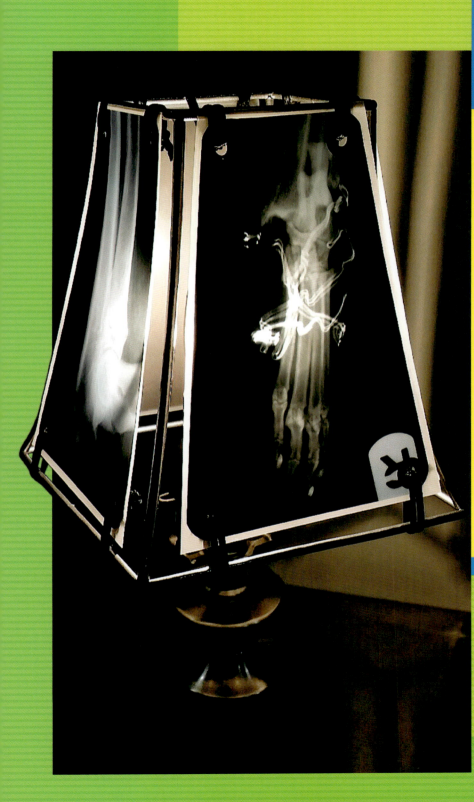

Q+A

Q How did you come up with the idea for animal X-ray lampshades?

A I had been collecting X-rays for many years and stumbled upon a small shop showcasing medical arts-related items with X-rays displayed in the window. Shortly after that, I was compelled to use some of my films to display, and using lamps seemed like the perfect medium.

Q Do you also do human X-ray lampshades?

A Yes, I have a small collection of human mostly pediatric X-rays. I've made one lamp and a couple night-lights with those so far.

Q Are all the X-rays and scans ones you have personally taken?

A Yes, in my 13 years as a veterinary technician, I have taken many of the X-rays in my collection.

Out of This World

HOME ALONE

BALLOON BILLBOARDS

Magician Rob Driscoll used his balloon artist talents to attempt a challenge: re-create one movie scene or poster out of balloons every week. The 41-year-old from Portsmouth, England, has been twisting balloons for more than 20 years and completed his popular yearlong photography series called "Twisted Cinema."

Far-Out Figurines

Rob Hull of Yorkshire, England, owns the world's largest collection of Daleks, extraterrestrial bad guys from the iconic British TV series *Doctor Who*. Rob has been building his 1,202-piece collection for 20 years. His stash even includes a six-foot-tall Dalek replica!

Tired Animals

Art From Steel, a company in Thailand, specializes in metal art. They recently created sculptures of lions and King Kong gorillas made from recycled tires! One of the tire lions is on display at the Ripley's Believe It or Not! Niagra Falls Odditorium.

Using the Force

Jump to Hypersleep

The force is with architect Peter McGowan. Peter built his son the birthday gift of any *Star Wars®* fan's dreams: a bed modeled after the cockpit of the *Millennium Falcon*. The rocket-ship sleeper, which took over a year to finish, features a wing that doubles as a writing desk and a massive hangar door that slides to cover the window.

The Ewok language is a combination of Tibetan and Nepalese.

Dutch and German speakers should have known Darth Vader was Luke's father from the beginning, as the Dutch and German words for father are "vader" and "Vater," respectively.

LOLLIPOP GUILD

California artist Matthew Carden plays with his food for a living, running an award-winning food photography studio with his wife, a chef and author. He also makes lollipop art so sweet, it might give you cavities. Matthew's tempting treats take the shape of pop icons such as Darth Vader, Mickey Mouse, and Hello Kitty.

The Little Things

ART ON TARGET

To promote world peace, California artist David Palmer created a series of portraits made entirely from bullets, including portraits of John Lennon, Abraham Lincoln, and John F. Kennedy. Palmer carefully arranged the bullet shell casings to craft his creations, which weigh 150 pounds apiece.

Each of the 4,500 cases that form this portrait of President Lincoln represents 150 men who died in the Civil War.

Pearl Portrait

Colombian artist Mateo Blanco spent six months creating a portrait of Elsa from Disney's *Frozen* out of more than 20,000 cupcake pearls! Mateo wanted to do something unique that kids would love, and he was inspired by the cute, little snowmen (called "snowgies") in *Frozen Fever*, the Disney short film. According to Mateo, the hardest part was getting the bouncy pearls to stay in place long enough for them to adhere to the background.

Mexican painter Cristiam Ramos re-creates artistic masterpieces on preserved butterfly wings, reproducing works by Monet, Van Gogh, Frida Kahlo, and other art masters.

You're watching TV. What are you most likely watching?

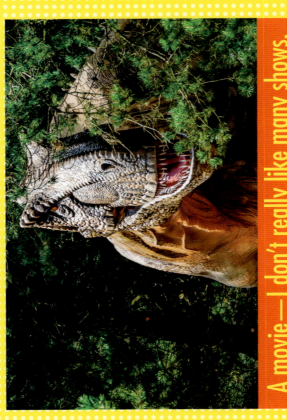

A movie—I don't really like many shows.

Anything with animals!

What is your dream job?

Doctor

Artist

What movies do you prefer to watch?

Popular older classics

Anything Disney!

Gaudí Submarine style
page 129

With X-ray lampshades
page 131

With an Elsa portrait
page 137

With a *Millennium Falcon* bed
page 134

Index

PHOTO CREDITS

Ripley Entertainment Inc. and the editors of this book wish to thank the following photographers, agents, and other individuals for permission to use and reprint the following photographs in this book. Any photographs included in this book that are not acknowledged below are property of the Ripley Archives. Great effort has been made to obtain permission from the owners of all material included in this book. Any errors that may have been made are unintentional and will gladly be corrected in future printings if notice is sent to Ripley Entertainment Inc., 7576 Kingspointe Parkway, Suite 188, Orlando, Florida 32819, USA.

COVER PHOTOS ©: lettuce: bryljaev/123RF; face: James Kuhn.

BACK COVER PHOTOS Pineapple head—Sherry Ma, Hansel Qiu; Ashima rock climbing—Brett Lowell / Reel Rock; Caroline Eriksson gingerbread art—Image provided by: Caroline Eriksson.

CONTENTS PAGE 2 Circuit board insects—Julie Alice Chappell; Amazing Neon Makeup—HID SAIB / CATERS NEWS; Elephant takes Amazing Selfie—CHRISTIAN LEBLANC / CATERS NEWS; 3 Volcano and Lightning Eruption—CATERS NEWS; Burger King Japan Samurai burgers—Burger King Japan, Inc.; Art on Track mobile garden—NOISEVELVET / CATERS NEWS

INTRO PAGE 7 Shogo Kawano skiing in samurai armor—Courtesy of Shogo Kawano; Pineapple head—Sherry Ma, Hansel Qiu; Squirrel Whisperer—Photo by Mary Krupa

CHAPTER 1 9 Cardboard Chuck Taylor converse—Michael Leavitt/REX Shutterstock; 10 Polymer clay book covers—Aniko Kolesnikova www.mandarin-duck.com E-mail: mymandarinducky@gmail.com; 10–11 Lego Tower World Record—Caters News; 12–13 Alina and Zollipops—Courtesy of Thomas F. Morse and Alina Morse, Zollipops; 14–15 Amazing Neon Makeup—HID SAIB / CATERS NEWS; 16 Starbucks coffee cup art—Courtesy of Creative Carrah; 17 MOSCOW, RUSSIA — JULY 7, 2012: Red pickup truck Ford F-150 Raptor at the city street—© Art Konovalov/Shutterstock.com; Macro of a Big Brown Cockroach eating crumbs—© Barnaby Chambers/Shutterstock.com; Coffee blender and boiler machine great for makes hot drinks—© John Kasawa/Shutterstock.com; Goldfish in aquarium isolated on white background—© Andrey Armyagov/Shutterstock.com; Tea in the wedding—© Mikhail_Kayl/Shutterstock.com; 18 Cardboard Box Wars—CAMPBELL MANDERSON / CATERS NEWS; 19 Cardboard stiletto—Michael Leavitt/REX Shutterstock; Cardboard Chuck Taylor converse—Michael Leavitt/REX Shutterstock; 20 2cm Tall Coffee Maker—IBERPRESS / CATERS NEWS; 21 Watermelon bagels—Courtesy of RocketNews24; Burger King Japan Samurai burgers—Burger King Japan, Inc.; 22 Batman cowl made from tree bark, France — Jul 2015: Christophe Guinet/REX Shutterstock; 23 Art on Track mobile garden—NOISEVELVET / CATERS NEWS; Boeing 747 Jumbo Jet Conference Table—Courtesy of MotoArt; 24 Couple's Willy Wonka Wedding Day—Caters News; Resignation cake and "sustainability" memo cake—Courtesy of Mark Herman; 26–27 Circuit board insects—Julie Alice Chappell; 28 Happy people jumping in Grand Canyon. Young multiethnic couple on hiking travel. Grand Canyon, south rim, Arizona, USA—© Maridav/Shutterstock.com; Teenager laughing, playing and fooling around on the Champ de Mars in front of the Eiffel Tower (La Tour Eiffel) in Paris—© kavalenkava volha/Shutterstock.com; 29 Full body length of a teenager walking—© Catalin Petolea/Shutterstock.com; A young tourist holding a map—© Michaelpuche/Shutterstock.com; Girl writes lying on the bed—© Artbox/Shutterstock.com; Smart and cheerful boy offering you a chocolate cookie. His arm is outstretched—© stockyimages/Shutterstock.com; Art on Track mobile garden—NOISEVELVET / CATERS NEWS; Cardboard Chuck Taylor converse—Michael Leavitt/REX Shutterstock; Alina and Zollipops—Courtesy of Thomas F. Morse and Alina Morse, Zollipops; Polymer clay book covers—Aniko Kolesnikova www.mandarin-duck.com E-mail: mymandarinducky@gmail.com

CHAPTER 2 31 Tractor Boy Stunts—UDAY DEOLEKAR / CATERS NEWS; 32 Real Life Forrest Gump—CATERS NEWS; Indiana Jane—SARAH LEE / CATERS NEWS; 33 One Legged rower—ANNE BERLIN / CATERS NEWS; 34–35 Shogo Kawano skiing in samurai armor—Courtesy of Shogo Kawano; 36 Dustin Murley falls off his ostrich as Jessey Sisson looks on during the ostrich race at the annual Ostrich Festival in Chandler, Arizona March 10, 2013—REUTERS/Joshua Lott; 37 Chess Boxing—RAY MORRIS-Hill / CATERS NEWS; 38–39 Balancing Artist Eskil Rønningsbakken—Sindre Lundvold / Barcroft Media / Getty Images; 40 Pineapple head—Sherry Ma, Hansel Qiu; 41 A Worker in biohazard suits hold a used Oil Containment boom as cleaning operations from a beach of Samet Island on July 31, 2013 in Rayong, Thailand—© Narongsak Nagadhana/Shutterstock.com; Bone structure—© sciencepics/Shutterstock.com; Happy female with Scottish flags on her cheeks, outdoor—© Michal Kowalski/Shutterstock.com; Cool Asian boy listening to music on headphones—© Hung Chung Chih/Shutterstock.com; 42–43 Superhero Post-it mural—Ben Brucker; 44–45 Ashima rock climbing—Brett Lowell / Reel Rock; 46 One Armed Golfer—CATERS NEWS; Girls Giant Tuna Catch—CATERS NEWS; 47 Tractor Boy Stunts—UDAY DEOLEKAR / CATERS NEWS; 48–49 Two men take part in traditional water jousting in the French southern city of Sète on August 20, 2011—PASCAL GUYOT/AFP/Getty Images; 50 (MOTION BLUR ON FEET AND BALL) young boy, football player doing amazing kick—© MANDY GODBEHEAR/Shutterstock.com; Young girl with drink watching TV in bed—© Cheryl Casey/Shutterstock.com; 51 Closeup portrait headshot nervous anxious stressed boy with eyeglasses biting fingernails looking anxiously craving something, afraid isolated grey wall background. Negative emotion facial expression—© PathDoc/Shutterstock.com; Happy hiker—Stock image—© awdebenham/iStock.com; Hand drawn superhero—© advent/Shutterstock.com; Fun laptop—© Alias Ching/Shutterstock.com; Girls Giant Tuna Catch—CATERS NEWS; Pineapple head—Sherry Ma, Hansel Qiu; Superhero Post-it mural—Ben Brucker; Ashima rock climbing—Brett Lowell / Reel Rock

CHAPTER 3 53 Once in a blue moon with detailed moon—© Beth Swanson/Shutterstock.com; 54 Massive beams of selenite dwarf explorers in the Cave of Crystals—CARSTEN PETER/ SPELEORESEARCH & FILMS/National Geographic Creative; 55 Glass beach at sunset — a former dump site, in which the glass has now become pebbles of sea glass. MacKerricher State Park. California. USA. January 2013:—© Floris van Breugel/naturepl.com; 56 Candlelit Vineyard—PAUL HEWITT PHOTOGRAPHY / CATERS NEWS; Frozen waves—Jonathan Nimerfroh www.jdnphotography.com; 57 Kiruna Winter Playground—Christian Strömqvist/PinPin Studio; 58–59 Natura Vive Skylodge Adventure Suites—Natura Vive; 59 Natura Vive Skylodge Adventure Suites—Natura Vive; 60–61 Volcano and Lightning Eruption—CATERS NEWS; 62–63 Milk carton igloo—Photo courtesy of Gary Burton; 64 Stuffed Toy Cafe—CATERS NEWS; 65 No Tie Restaurant—PINNACLE PEAK PATIO / CATERS NEWS; 66 APTOPIX GUATEMALA SINKHOLE—ASSOCIATED PRESS; 67 Huge hurricane between Florida and Cuba. Elements of this image furnished by NASA—© Harvepino/Shutterstock.com; Long exposure, Tungurahua volcano with blue skyes—© Fotos593/Shutterstock.com; Once in a blue moon with detailed moon—© Beth Swanson/Shutterstock.com; Sunflower with blue sky and beautiful sun / sunflower—© PhotographyByMK/Shutterstock.com; Oak tree with green leaves on a background of the night sky and the Milky Way—© AlexussK/Shutterstock.com; Lightning in Front of a Dramatic Background—© Olaf Naami/Shutterstock.com; 68–69 World's Biggest Cave—John Spies / Barcroft Media; 70 Dragon Trees at Socotra Island in Yemen—The Asahi Shimbun via Getty Images; 71 INDIA-RELIGION-SOCIETY-CRIME—PUNIT PARANJPE/AFP/Getty Images; Archstoyanie Festival Russia—KARLI LUIK / CATERS NEWS; 72 Swimming Race Teenager Swimming race boy teen breastroke style race—© ChrisVanLennepPhoto/Shutterstock.com; Hiker woman. Hiking asian woman walking with hiking poles and hiking backpack smiling happy outdoors in nature. Hiker in background—© Maridav/Shutterstock.com; 73 Girl Reading Book With Flashlight Under The Blanket On Bed—© Andrey_Popov/Shutterstock.com; Boy with Digital Tablet — Stock image—© Sasa Dinic/iStock.com; Jumping girl with autumn leaves — Stock image—© 3sbworld/iStock.com; Smiling teenager girl holding white pear flowers — Stock image—© SerrNovik/iStock.com; World's Biggest Cave—John Spies / Barcroft Media; Natura Vive Skylodge Adventure Suites—Natura Vive; Kiruna Winter Playground—Christian Strömqvist/PinPin Studio; Glass beach at sunset — a former dump site, in which the glass has now become pebbles of sea glass. MacKerricher State Park. California. USA. January 2013—© Floris van Breugel/naturepl.com

CHAPTER 4 75 Blue dragon (glaucus atlanticus)—© Sylke Rohrlach, Wikimedia Commons // CC-BY-SA 2.0; 76 Stork Heart Bird—INGRID BUNSE / CATERS NEWS; 77 Guy walks his pet tortoise around the streets of Tokyo—© Exclusivepix Media; 78 Swimming with Beasts—JEREMY FERRIS / CATERS NEWS; 79 Elephant takes Amazing Selfie—CHRISTIAN LEBLANC / CATERS NEWS; Squirrel weights—MAX ELLIS / CATERS NEWS; 80 Alien spider—ROBERT WHYTE / CATERS NEWS; 81 Insect protein bars—Photos shot by Axel Sigurðarson "Jungle Bar"; Dust mites in a pillow—© Juan Gaertner/Shutterstock.com; Bird-dropping spider — Stock image—© suwwch/iStock.com; Weta on rock—© Kim Howell/Shutterstock.com; Leaf cutter ant — Stock image—© michaklootwijk/iStock.com; 82 Shrimp Dentist—TIM LAMAN / CATERS NEWS; 83 Californian Freediver Catches Then Releases Giant Lobster—Forrest Galante / Barcroft USA; Broken neck giraffe—MARK DRYSDALE / CATERS NEWS; 84–85 Squirrel Whisperer—Photo by Mary Krupa; 86–87 Mongolian tribe who rely on Reindeers — Jun 2014—Pascal Mannaerts/REX Shutterstock; 88–89 Bird caught in spider's web—Isak Pretorius—theafricanphotographer.com; 90–91 Paw Star Game Kitten Baseball—CROWN MEDIA UNITED STATES / CATERS NEWS; 92 CHINA NANJING HAIRY CRAB VENDING MACHINE—Wen bao — Imaginechina via AP Images; 93 Blue dragon (glaucus atlanticus)—© Sylke Rohrlach, Wikimedia Commons // CC-BY-SA 2.0; 94 View of Manhattan New York City Skyline Buildings from High Rise Window — Beautiful Expensive Real Estate overlooking Empire State Building and Skyscrapers in Gorgeous Breathtaking Penthouse Cityscape—© stockelements/Shutterstock.com; Cottage at the lake—© LesPalenik/Shutterstock.com; 95 Mess in bedroom — Stock image—© Figure8Photos/iStock.com; Stylish modern white room with blue details—© Photographee.eu/Shutterstock.com; Let's make this a cute one — Stock image—© gradyreese/iStock.com; Education concept – group of students at school—© Syda Productions/Shutterstock.com; Portrait of happy teen girls showing thumbs up isolated one white—© Subbotina Anna/Shutterstock.com; Blue dragon (glaucus atlanticus)—© Sylke Rohrlach, Wikimedia Commons // CC-BY-SA 2.0; Elephant takes Amazing Selfie—CHRISTIAN LEBLANC / CATERS NEWS; Alien spider—ROBERT WHYTE / CATERS NEWS; Squirrel weights—MAX ELLIS / CATERS NEWS

CHAPTER 5 97 Bacteria Handprint—Any use or display of the Content shall be accompanied by a legible trademark notice equivalent to "TM Tasha Sturm" or "® Tasha Sturm."; 100–101 Bajau people of Malaysia—Ng Choo Kia/HotSpot Media; 102 Wheelchair action hero—DAN ROWLANDS/MERCURY PRESS; 103 No-Armed Fisherman—PRO FISHING MANAGEMENT / CATERS NEWS; 104 Chinese dancing teacher Tian Jiashi puts a live spider into his mouth in Changchun city, northeast China's Jilin province, 18 November 2015—Imaginechina; 105 James Kuhn, who is painting his face differently every day for 365 days—James Kuhn/REX/Shutterstock; 106 Neptune underwater headphones—Filis/BNPS; 107 Microwave oven isolated on white background—© Oleksiy Mark/Shutterstock.com; Teen listening music wearing headphones—© MANDY GODBEHEAR/Shutterstock.com; Macro shot of a 100 dollar—© JIANG HONGYAN/Shutterstock.com; Space shuttle taking off on a mission—© Fer Gregory/Shutterstock.com; MARYLAND,USA — MAY 15: Vending Machine at a Hospital in Maryland, USA on May 15, 2013—© Lissandra Melo/Shutterstock.com; 108–109 Tadas Maksimovas — playing violin with human hair for strings—Concept: Tadas Maksimovas, Music: Eimantas Belickas, Hair: Tadas Maksimovas, Camera: Giedrius Jurkonis, Kęstutis Kurienius, Styling: Ieva Sereikytė, Animation: Andrius Alčiauskas, Song: Everyday to the War (Kasdien į Karą) by AIRIJA, Images: Linas Justice; 110–111 Anatomical Art—LISA NILSSON / JOHN POLAK / CATERS NEWS; 112–113 Bacteria Handprint—Any use or display of the Content shall be accompanied by a legible trademark notice equivalent to "TM Tasha Sturm" or "® Tasha Sturm"; 114 Richie Streate's UV Tattoos—Courtesy of Richie Streate; 115 Human hair insects—Adrienne Antonson; 116 Boy surfing in the waves with skim board—© Luis Louro/Shutterstock.com; Happy girl relaxing in the water—© Nejron Photo/Shutterstock.com; 117 Teacher Helping Pupil To Play Trumpet In Music Lesson—© SpeedKingz/Shutterstock.com; Male Pupil In High School Art Class—© Monkey Business Images/Shutterstock.com; Young woman hiding behind a book—© Piotr Marcinski/Shutterstock.com; Classmate pupils running outside. — Stock image—© skynesher/iStock.com; James Kuhn, who is painting his face differently every day for 365 days — Oct 2008 I'm all ears!—James Kuhn/REX/Shutterstock; Tadas Maksimovas — playing violin with human hair for strings—Concept: Tadas Maksimovas, Music: Eimantas Belickas, Hair: Tadas Maksimovas, Camera: Giedrius Jurkonis, Kęstutis Kurienius, Styling: Ieva Sereikytė, Animation: Andrius Alčiauskas, Song: Everyday to the War (Kasdien į Karą) by AIRIJA, Images: Linas Justice; Wheelchair action hero—DAN ROWLANDS/MERCURY PRESS; Anatomical Art—LISA NILSSON / JOHN POLAK / CATERS NEWS

CHAPTER 6 119 Matthew Carden's "Pop Icons" series—© Matthew Carden; 120 MarvelHous Make up artist—NEIL ZELLER/ LIANNE MOSELEY / CATERS NEWS; 121 An assistant of Chinese fine arts teacher Xing Yile tests the models of Iron Man and Hulkbuster armors they made at the underground parking lot of Zhengzhou 106 Middle School in Zhengzhou city, central China's Henan province, 12 May 2015—Imaginechina; 122–123 Caroline Eriksson gingerbread art—Image provided by: Caroline Eriksson; 124 School Delorean Car—ANDY BARNES/ CATERS NEWS; 125 Frozen Car—CATERS NEWS AGENCY; 126 Giant Flying V Guitar—Photo courtesy of The National GUITAR Museum; 127 Skateboard Instruments—Juhana Nyrhinen and www.masauniverse.tumblr.com; Siberian Forest Cat at the Piano—© Kathleen Coffler/Shutterstock.com; CEO and founder of Apple Computers & Pixar boss, STEVE JOBS, at the world premiere of Disney/Pixar's Monsters, Inc., at the El Capitan Theatre, Hollywood. 28OCT2001. Paul Smith/Featureflash—© Featureflash/Shutterstock.com; Audio cassette and tape composition—© The_Pixel/Shutterstock.com; Premature baby boy in Intensive Care Unit at hospital—© Steve Lovegrove/Shutterstock.com; 128 GIRL MAKES SOAPS FOR GEEKS — DIGITAL SOAPS / MERCURY PRESS / CATERS NEWS; RUBBER DUCK COLLECTOR—MERCURY PRESS / CATERS NEWS; 129 Gaudi Submarine bathroom—Anthony Lindsey Photography; 130–131 X-ray lamps—spike@xrayvisiondesigns.com; 131 X-ray lamps create—Spike Vain—A YaQuB Flick; 132 Balloon Art (Home Alone)—CATERS NEWS; BALLOON ART MOVIE (Nightmare Before Christmas)—CATERS NEWS; 133 Biggest Dalek Collection—MIKEY JONES / CATERS NEWS; 134 Star Wars bed—Ed McGowan / PlainJoe Studios; 135 Matthew Carden's "Pop Icons" series—© Matthew Carden; 138 Brown bear on Alaska—© Galyna Andrushko/Shutterstock.com; GIVSKUD, DENMARK — MAY 1 – 2015: Tyrannosaurus Rex at the dinosaur theme park at Givskud Zoo—© Polarpx/Shutterstock.com; 139 13NOV99: "Toy Story" character BUZZ LIGHTYEAR at the world premiere of Disney/Pixar's "Toy Story 2" at the El Capitan Theatre, Hollywood. Paul Smith / Featureflash—© Featureflash/Shutterstock.com; UNITED STATES – CIRCA 1990: a postage stamp printed in USA showing an image of Gone With the Wind film, circa 1990—© catwalker/Shutterstock.com; Side view of young artist with brush and palette is going to painting a picture—© Vgstockstudio/Shutterstock.com; Group of medical workers portrait in hospital—© michaeljung/Shutterstock.com; Gaudi Submarine bathroom—Anthony Lindsey Photography; X-ray lamps—spike@xrayvisiondesigns.com; Star Wars bed—Ed McGowan / PlainJoe Studios

144